Daniel Deleanu

Poems in the Language Of Shakespeare

LogoStar Press

Toronto

ISBN: 978-1-105-57065-0

Printed and bound in the USA.

CONTENTS

I Thank the Fledged[1] Arrows

I thank the fledged arrows in the air
For the fortunes of thy likeness,
I shall assume honour in thy desert,
Glean'd to cozened[2] natures,
As heaven's treasure-houses withal[3] fear
Prove of love's villainy'n'despair.

Fond was she of all celestial beauties,
Hindering the flow of poison in the heart,
Obscur'd is now the tongue and eye,
And to certainty thoughts are wont[4] no more.

Beshrew[5] Cupid's blush, he that's gilded,
In exactions of fortuity[6] and to my soul
Constant companion, torch-bearer, and foe.

O thought express disabling of myself,
In forms grav'd in quaint immur'd gems,
Her bare breast a saint's meagre[7] shrine.

---

[1] Fledged – equipped with feathers
[2] Cozened – cheated
[3] Withal – with this
[4] Wont – accustomed to
[5] Beshrew – curse, imprecate, wish evil
[6] Fortuity – accidental occurrence, chance
[7] Meagre – small-scaled

A Perfect Visitation

Word perfectness
Is love's gentle visitation,
For your fair approach has sworn
No ignorance, and in its gentle courts,
It so beseemeth me,[8]
My darling soul,
I will be welcomed and truly garnished
With your curtsy[9] and your love.

My eyes in beholding thee
Are by fine hap no common,
So what's this merry choler's
Purchase in the cap,
And complimented,
How does it jig off a tune from you,
From upon whose lips
I make so passionate a hearing?

A snip and away, give enlargement
To my passion festinately[10] now,
My mouth let enchanted be
With the glassed tend'ring of a kiss!

An unpeopled house,
So unbedecked with pride and praise
Is my heart without you,
For as it is, here and now,
Pathetical and native it does owe
The green and vary wit,

---

[8] Beseemeth me – seems to me
[9] Curtsy – surrender
[10] Festinately – quickly, swiftly

And the passado[11] of love subdued.
The rest is fair weather after you.

[11] A fencing maneuver in which the foil is thrust forward and one foot advanced

Labouring in Love

Her passions are like winter's end,
Or like a worthy crown of fire air-drawn,
Scores of mortal murders in my heart,
Those that in the clouds we bury
Can nod, but cannot ever speak.

A dismal, alas, distilled by magic thought,
And 'bove the chiefest foes of mischance
That grace us when they're done to death[12]
Is what makes an angel's walk
From th' gates of hell to heaven's courts.

Labour in love's care shall avail,
Contemptuous like a hangman's sweat.
For her passions are like winter's dreams,
To the soul minion[13] and blessed anon.[14]

Love is verily an imperfect speaker,
For it never the truth unfolds:
But thou canst, as breath into a gust,
Stand within the prospect of perfect silence
As long as thou thyself dost make
Nothing afeard of what with love
Thou truly with beauty ornament.

---

[12] Done to death – put to death
[13] Minion – favourite
[14] Anon – soon

Shrewdly Out of Circumstance[15]

That which is lost be not found:
With mere conceit and less bravery,
An overtone of morbid affectation
Bids speed fortune to what's most humane,
And thus which hazard o'ercharged
With the luxuries of fate tardied[16]
That nature's very practice has revealed.
And then Apollo with his thankful trifles
Wardens Dionysus, the drunken snapper-up,
And puts him in the stocks of time
I'th'name of Zeus and his boyish altos[17]
That lay it on in the springe[18] of poison,
The unconsidered history of a departure
Dished with no return, nor with the moiety[19]
Of a truly hopeful and buoyant conscience.
And then for spare, to cry "Fie!"[20]
Upon the dominion of all heaven's mercy
And commend[21] it wisely to some realm
Wherein death, 'tis prayed, may either
Humour it or purblindly[22] end it.

---

15 Out of circumstance – out of arguments, defeated in a debate
16 Tardied – unwary, unready
17 Altos – singers
18 Springe – snare
19 Moiety – portion
20 Fie! – Shame on you!
21 Commend – send
22 Purblindly – completely blindly

Trothplight[23]

In death's silent conference
There is no sleeping ground,
But the manners of beshrew[24] and pride.
So, ere[25] thou wak'st
From thy unstirring night
In eternity's wanton[26] mazes,
Look for me anon[27] beneath thy eyelid,
And offer me, while still asleep,
Thy amiable[28] and curst[29] coy.[30]

And if, my Princess dear, thou hearken
Moused[31] words like quailing[32] music
Coming from unparted lips,
Know that the Furies' thread'n'thrum[33]
Have painted your pap[34] and cheer[35]
In the colour of the confounded moon.

And now, quell[36] me, if thou wilst,
For death shall find me
By bootless[37] moonshine, not starlight,

---

[23] Trothplight – the act of becoming engaged or married
[24] Beshrew – curse, imprecate, wish evil
[25] Ere – before
[26] Wanton – luxurious
[27] Anon – soon
[28] Amiable – lovely
[29] Curst – cursed
[30] Coy – touch, caress
[31] Moused – prowled
[32] Quailing – Frightening
[33] Thread'n'thrum – good and evil together
[34] Pap – breast
[35] Cheer – countenance, expression, face
[36] Quell – kill

So let my heart want no more
And fill up with mud,
And in the hoary-headed ringlet[38] of frost
Let thy steps for aye[39] trace
The welkin's[40] snuffing[41] pomp.

---

[37] Bootless – unprofitable, useless
[38] Ringlet – dance in a circle
[39] For eye – forever
[40] Welkin – sky
[41] Snuffing – scoffing, despising

Cure for a Deadly Woe

The impression of a prologue in my brain
Must arbitrate true soldiership:
Who is more politic[42] in adoration –
The decayer of a cruel trade
Of reechy[43] deeds and dear concernings,[44]
Or the felicity's enactures[45] both here and hence[46]?
And, as such, 'twere good you comprehend
The scourge and blessing of a prating[47] potency
Wherein one catches
The muted audience of a soul in love.

With wings encumb'red,[48] the angel is no dove,
And more relative than this
Is the horror fouled and in unwisdom unabashed;
Thus hitherto doth truth to heaven wed
And doth pursue me a bond of fate:
So glass-gazing[49] is a breath in pain,
When Cupid, for the furnishing[50] of love,
Shall neither o'ercrow[51] nor tremble.

---

[42] Politic – prudent
[43] Reechy – filthy
[44] Dear concernings – important personal matters
[45] Enactures – fulfillments
[46] Hence – in the next world
[47] Prating – chattering
[48] Encumb'red – folded
[49] Glass-gazing – conceited, narcissistic
[50] Furnishing – pretext
[51] O'ercrow – triumph over

The Sonnet of Autumn

A benediction, most miraculous,
As only in the double[52] broil of fate
Nature can, in a fastidious addition,
Present the horror of its time when false.[53]

Nimbly,[54] dawn's light carves out its passage
According to the gift of a bounteous nature:
Hail, friend, in my eye thou art incarnadine[55]
Like fire in a crucible's procreant cradle.[56]

As thou didst, in such an honour named,
Thy hour shall be anon[57] a large spread of time –
Even furbished[58] words will never grasp it.

The new guest of summer hath a pleasant seat,
To which, alas, she giveth not the cheer,
Nor doth she show her untitled grieving eyes.

---

[52] Double – two-faced
[53] False – unreal
[54] Nimbly – gently, sweetly
[55] Incarnadine – dye blood-red
[56] Procreant cradle – nest for a bird's young
[57] Anon – soon
[58] Furbished – well-prepared

An Unacquainted Counsel

To mingle the copy of a charitable smile
With the hindrance of the gazing branches,
To charge the tongue-tied wonders
Of an unacquainted counsel
With the swainly[59] posterity of history's liege,
I prithee,[60] O sweet breeze of love,
Pawn[61] not thy last hour which thou hath
To undergo so horrendous, so improper,
An alt'ration of thy wanton[62] heart.

And then death, that sacred mighty bond,
Let thou seal thy irremovable[63] lot;
And hence, more ponderous,[64]
Omit the courtesy due the living,
And purchase[65] for thyself
The unfledged[66] heartiness[67]
Of the fasting[68] eternal night.

---

[59] Swainly – boyish, young
[60] Prithee – pray thee, ask you kindly, please
[61] Pawn – risk
[62] Wanton – playful, frolicsome
[63] Irremovable – immovable, fixed, unchangeable
[64] More ponderous – very serious
[65] Purchase – procure
[66] Unfledged – immature, innocent
[67] Heartiness – peaceful joy
[68] Fasting – empty, voided

Dispensation for an Oath

Now fair befall[69] to the cipher
Of good wit and shaded[70] reason,
Mighty-jointed Hercules himself
Could not beseech to challenge
An oracle to whom
No one even heeds attention.

Methinks I should thereby
Set thee down, fate, and forgive
Thy strangeness[71] and thy glozes.[72]

It is sacred duty to be thus forsworn,
For if thou dost not love encounter
In the embraces of a transgressing heart,
Thou shalt heavily be punished
Behind the other world's
Humours and forbidden gates.

But thy kiss is a prodigal[73] banquet,
Upon whose illustrious attendance
I turn into the meek embassy[74]
Of endless love, whose subtle voice
Is rooted in the Hesperiades'[75] garden,

---

[69] Fair befall – good luck
[70] Shaded – hidden
[71] Strangeness – originality
[72] Glozes – clever comments
[73] Prodigal – lavish
[74] Embassy – message
[75] The last of the twelve labours of Hercules was to obtain the golden apples from a tree growing in the garden oh Hesperus, which was guarded by his daughters, the Hesperides, and by a fierce dragon.

Where out of heart, and out of grace,
Reins the potent legged serpent,
The welkin's regental deputy.[76]

[76] Welkin's regental deputy – heaven's assistant governor (welkin = sky, heavens; regental = governing, leading)

They Hail Thee Bounteous

They hail thee bounteous
Whereby thou dost not deceive,
And worse hath not yet commenced.

Thy reechy[77] silence though doth cautel[78]
When tenable[79] in the clamour of a whip
Whose sealed[80] passion candied is
In the ungalled[81] fullness of the absolute.

And then thou sleep, confessed but unproved,
This chanced soliciting[82] all fantastical in shape
And in contents too abhorred to be bred.

Thou speak'st with all thy charm,
And I, a homely[83] man,
Devoid of eloquence'n'wit,
Stubborn[84] and unruly,
From every word thou pronouncest
I make a truth to whose fatal vision
I succumb, an uninvested[85] king
Of the uncompounded[86] night eternal.

---

[77] Reechy – unclean, impure
[78] Cautel – betray
[79] Tenable – firmly held
[80] Sealed – marked
[81] Ungalled – peaceful, serene
[82] Soliciting – invitation
[83] Homely – plain, simple
[84] Stubborn – rude
[85] Invested – crowned
[86] Uncompounded – uncreated

Beseech Thy Lot

Beseech thy lot to dry not
Thy remedies for life,
For death's petitions no anchor hold!
And in th' promotion that follows after,
May thy obedience to thy master
Hover over th' silent running glass[87]
For time, being dead,
Neither takes bargain nor ever shall.

Again virginalling[88] and practising smiles
In a torrid looking-glass as 'twere
Narcissus' wantonness[89] in a pool of water?
They say the sea is a copy of the sky
Made i'th' name of the daffodils
Which garland the neck of night,
Whose fortune is an oracle fulfilled
And a foe's pregnant[90] recognition
Of the merciful fail[91] of man
In the garden that's called Eden.

And then, to what avail the absence
That foretells the highness of th' hour
If it forwarns not the unthought place
Whereto one goes, cap-à-pie,[92]
Neither ponderous nor discontenting?[93]

---

[87] Running glass – hourglass
[88] Virginalling – playing the virginals
[89] Wantonness – playfulness, frolicsomeness
[90] Pregnant – evident, clear
[91] Fail – failure
[92] Cap-à-pie – from head to foot
[93] Discontenting – discontented

A Poem on Betrayal

I shall put a garland round about[94] thy heart,
Dulcet[95] and unquenched as thy very mouth,
When with it to kiss me thou canst not,
Absorbed in thy maiden's unstreaked[96] office.[97]

Caress me now asleep against thy reverie,
And let the clamorous cloud clouding my vision
Wither my warrior's soul to a stolen death,
And 'noint my dreamful eye with love, not slumber.

The riot of thy lips, like death, is a nuptial grace
Masqued as an abridgement that restoreth amends,[98]
An orgy ending in plainsong and in silence.
O heaven, this is my heart here that lieth asleep,
A cloistered shadow that in the dream of death
Hast abjured the world, its recreants,[99] and yoke.

---

[94] Round about – a pleonastic form of "(a)round" or "about" often used by Shakespeare
[95] Dulcet – sweet, melodious
[96] Unstreaked – unanointed, puny, trivial
[97] Office – business, thing, deed; unstreaked office – puny things, trifles
[98] Restoreth amends – gives satisfaction in return
[99] Recreant – betrayer

Of Sorriest Conjurations

In the vessel of my utterance
Dwell a fruitless crown and barren sceptre,
A conference that's not under fortune
When it doth torture the still heavens nightly:
Nought is had,[100] nought is regarded.[101]

With my drowsy hand I shall start anon[102]
To streak the light and scarf up the moon,
Spurring the day away apace[103] at last
To make room for the lated[104] guest:
The remembrancer of a gracious fit
Whose faith is a vouched[105] mischance.[106]
I shall spurn all that was not born yet,
And in the gracious sleep of fate
I shall trust nevermore:
I'll resolve with a little spirit[107]
The things that have been oddly handled,
And in a foggy cloud I shall find my wake.[108]

Then it shall be morn[109] again,
And mine honours upon lot's aid[110]
Shall be the fortified purge of death.

---

[100] Nought is had – nothing has been gained
[101] Nought is regarded – everything is ignored
[102] Anon – soon
[103] Apace – quickly
[104] Lated – belated
[105] Vouched – commended by courtesy
[106] Mischance – bad luck
[107] A little spirit – a familiar spirit
[108] Wake – call to arms
[109] Morn – morning, dawn
[110] Mine honours upon lot's aid – the honours conferred by fate upon me

Opprobrium to a Most Common Dream

Waiting for thy purblind[111] caresses,
Whisp'ring the revolted[112] words whose gambols
Are rounding[113] of unconsidered trifles,
You appear to me as an angel I've acquainted
In the unfledgèd[114] hours of the night.

Of all else, make proselytes
Betimes[115] of those like me,
Who boast of the wanton[116] death
In the lost[117] bed of life.

And I am questioned by thy graces, not my fears,
Of the quenched zeal that builds
The tuneful blush of an unsullied mark
By destiny in vain obscured
And by thy presence gloriously pranked up.

Masks for the heart of steel that unpromised
Shouldst take no heed of me
I've seen one fardel[118] in a million;
But extempore[119] thou only
Giveth me the sweet pleasure and kind hope
To preserve myself in being.[120]

---

[111] Purblind – utterly blind
[112] Revolted – faithless
[113] Are rounding – are talking secretly
[114] Unfledged – immature, inexperienced, young
[115] Betimes – soon
[116] Wanton – lascivious, playful, frolicsome
[117] Lost – dead
[118] Fardel – bundle
[119] Extempore – without foresight
[120] To preserve myself in being – to stay alive

Giving Thanks for Nought

'Tide[121] leviathan[122] of the sea of sorrow!
How sweet to faint with light in the eyelid's
Courtesy of sleep and its grievous sigh,
Wherein one glance will serve
As sandy turf for both of us.

Through the distance have I gone,
Where silence is fed the night
And the day's beshrew[123]
Is an oath of death and life.
Be it so then, my love, let thy shadow[124]
Further the waggish[125] glass[126] yet off.

Belike[127] time uncoils in want of love,
So tame thy desire!
Vow[128] for aye[129] destiny's esteem!
The kinder death, to give life
Thanks for simply nought.
The kinder us, to take as blemish
The consecrate[130] midst of a rotten phrase.

Newly bent in the heavens,
The Milky Way is grown so foul:

---

[121] 'Tide – betide, come
[122] Leviathan – sea monster
[123] Beshrew – curse
[124] Likeness – representation
[125] Waggish – playful, mischievous
[126] Glass – mirror
[127] Belike – very likely
[128] Vow – protest
[129] For aye – forever
[130] Consecrate – consecrated

The neaf[131] of Hercules himself
Could not uncurve it,
Not even in the gleek[132] of a grunt
That makes one die afeared,
Wilfully in the melody
Of the wode[133] hate of man,
Like weaving spiders
In the childing[134] nest
Of a pelting[135] autumn hour.[136]

---

[131] Neaf – fist
[132] Gleek – scoff, jest
[133] Wode (pronounced like "wood") – mad
[134] Childing – fruitful
[135] Pelting – paltry, insignificant
[136] Autumn hour – autumn day

A Spruceful Ostentation

If my hand be out, then just
Challenge it to beg and clown,
And edge the schedule of the world
With a word unmortified and unresolved
So that I hereupon may confess
That with thou I am in love!

So thou shalt know what girdles truth,
For this intimateth[137] him whose scorn for it
Is greater than the unpeopled house of God
Ere he made this piece of sea a land;
As for the immured[138] honour of thy name,
Merry, how could I contemplate its song
As long as its thrice-told tale
Hath not yet, alas mine mind, even arrived
At the ears that make the lips proud heirs
To thy most humble of affections?

This spruceful ostentation is not over yet,
But entirely to my hests[139] left to demand
That which had depart withal[140]
The soul's yielding make me tender of[141]
To do my commendations[142] and farewells,
Heart-lodged in the truth of the sun's flare.

---

[137] Intimateth – refers, tells, informs
[138] Immured – walled-up
[139] Hests – orders
[140] Had depart withal – would part with
[141] Make me tender of – offer me
[142] To do my commendations – to give my greetings

The Cankerblossom's[143] Ballad

Methought that conceived was I
In the tuned[144]beauty of thy truth,
And in the joyous faith of thy love;
But, verily, I was wholly wrong:
I did approve[145] love's conference,
But in the vainglory of tomorrow's flight
It ne'er shall be more than the sleeping lie
Of an untranslated[146] and wanton[147] lore.

I once hailed down words that weren't mine,
And in the stealth of life I discover'd death:
In my extenuating protests[148] I sighed blood
And cheered like a babe without a face
In the minding[149] games of love.[150]

Hence, here I stand and condole:[151]
I am the heresy of fairy toys[152]
And empty orbs[153] that all saints leave
When they depart this world.

---

[143] Cankerblossom – worm that destroys the flower bud
[144] Tuned – melodious
[145] Approve – test
[146] Untranslated – untransformed
[147] Wanton – tricky
[148] Protests – vows
[149] Minding – intending
[150] Games – jests
[151] Condole – lament
[152] Fairy toys – trifling tales about fairies
[153] Orbs – circles, halos

A Cradle and a Swelling Act[154]

This cradle has a pleasant frieze,
A coin of vantage[155] with hell underneath,
And a verdant piece of heaven on top of it:
Conduct me to mine Celestial Host, thee I pray,
Lead mine soul upon thy very aid[156]
To the unaccounted graceful banquets
Sung of i' th' most sublime of the adages![157]

This cradle has a pleasant frieze
Made, even as the greatest kings' sceptres,
From the dust of the fell[158] grief with which
Tomorrow bestows upon the world
A joy that is an acquiescent invention[159]
And therewithal,[160] a bodement[161] ne'er told.

Therefore, sleep mine soul,
Rest well in thy dusty cradle
Which pains no more the procreator
Of his eternal starless night,
A baby with a plenteous dark infinity
Growing in its hollow eyes
And with limbs of frantic worms.

---

[154] Swelling act – unfolding drama
[155] Coin of vantage – suitable corner
[156] Upon thy aid – on your behalf
[157] Adage – poem, song
[158] Fell – fierce, deadly
[159] Invention – story, tale
[160] Therewithal – with all that, besides
[161] Bodement – prophecy

As the Earth Sees Worship Fresh

As the earth sees worship fresh[162]
Better than the distrust of heaven,
I wish the dust more orisons[163] know
Than the sorrows that lodge
In its accursed and vain belly.

A man hath been publicly accused
Of the absence of grief, and love,
The tongue-tied scourge from the stars
That hamstrings the cogitation of all lies,
Didst incite the peaceful reverence
Of the irremovable[164] blood boasted
By the great Zeus and his priest,
So filled with fortune's hazards.

Hence, amazedly unto thee I speak,
I, the prophet of fragile bliss,
And both graceful[165] and damnable
I behold from the most worst[166]
How I become one with the marvel
Of my very meaning
Fading in a cloud of mist.

---

[162] Fresh – pure, wholesome
[163] Orisons – prayers
[164] Irremovable – unmoving, not flowing
[165] Graceful – full of grace
[166] The superlative is doubled for stylistic emphasis (poetic licence based on a pleonasm)

If Heaven Is

If heaven is an abode only for good carriage,[167]
Then, tell me, I beg of thee, what of hell?

Who therefore is to stay in awe thanksgiving
When the realm of eternal death is a living art?

If the obedient countenance makes
The ebb and flow of turtles'[168] love peremptory[169]
As the eagle-sighted angels in the skies,
Then to whom do we owe this inspired fury[170]
Whose grace-filled breath is so much wished?

I, by my troth,[171] seek a dispensation of my vow,[172]
Hence, pardon me, if I am too sudden bold,[173]
But please let me enter this unpeopled dwelling
Whose desolation is most pleasant if
Before its passado[174] I can, one more time,
In my cormorant[175] arms, Princess, hold thee tight.

---

[167] Carriage – behaviour
[168] Turtles – turtledoves, lovers
[169] Peremptory – overbearing
[170] Inspired fury – poetic frenzy
[171] By my troth – I swear, I give you my word
[172] Vow – spiritual pledge, oath
[173] Bold – rude, impolite
[174] Before its passado – before entering it
[175] Cormorant – (adj.) ravenous

In the Reach of Thy Arms

All the pride that I employ to win,
All the aloof and disdainful sorrow,
No matter how much coy or demure,
Is the mystery of fire, hence not in vain,
Nor its fearful bodements[176] trills of love.

Dwell the heavens in a cage of words,
The privacy of thy soul is now
By myriads of mortal thoughts[177] invaded.

Give thy raw[178] hand to me,
And in the palace of thy bosom,
Beguile the time[179] and make span[180]
For the dispatch[181] of my illusion!

But, alas, the heart hath slammed shut,
So dawn shall ne'er again be drawn
On the unveiled skin of the world.

---

[176] Bodements – prophecies
[177] Mortal thoughts – also means "thoughts of death"
[178] Raw – young
[179] Beguile the time – deceive the world
[180] Make span – make room
[181] Dispatch – putting to death, execution

Sonnet for a Princess

Art thou, Princess, ashen[182] for tiredness, or love?
For amongst the stars there is a joyless constancy
Which in the meanderings of a shapeless sky
Created a weary mass wrapp'd in a gauzy cloak
That caused the moon's shadow totter forth.
Shall I weigh thee against the world's declines?
Shall I balance thee instead on the bud of eternity?
Thy breath[183] charmeth mine pitiable hearing oft,
Thy love wodes[184] my poor wits and heart
Until, of faults attainted,[185] I scorn myself of vile
With fate's vantage[186] no more acquainted.
So here I lie now unconcealed but forsworn.[187]
And only the moon's shadow is music to my ears,
For it alone, Princess, glows ev'n as thy face.

---

[182] Ashen – pale
[183] Breath – voice
[184] Wodes (pronounced "woods") – maddens
[185] Attainted – disgraced
[186] Vantage – advantage, favour
[187] Forsworn – denied, abandoned

A Trembled Censure

The crackling stars darkling in a night's quietude
Will perchance one day remind thee of my sorrows
And thus, in the blazing hour of thine sleep,
You shall challenge[188] thyself with the tryst
Of he whose curse cast himself down upon the pyre
Of a tombless dream enshrined like a feeble gasp
In the famish'd flesh of the inglorious lips
That did not touch the juggling[189] arc of thy mouth.

Hie![190] Forgive thyself, for the deed is done,
And from within the mass of carcasses and all sorts
Of stagnant tides and other lifeless things,
Build for me a wholesome temple of seasonless
Chaos whose silent depths are sealed with thy kiss.

The world is void without thee, and with thee
Is ne'er full; all degrees are but one thought,
And that herbless thought's a word thou didst have:
To say in silence of love a sentence which indeed
Is producing forth[191] a recompense in boons of gold
For three words which to me thou didst ne'er utter.

---

[188] Challenge – blame
[189] Juggling – deceitful
[190] Hie! – Hurry!
[191] Producing forth – seeking out

An Exhortation, Not a Lament

Trembles the hoar of thy prime,
So the flesh of spring takes flight no longer:
On the final steps of dark thou art thc head
Of the last dream of grief, and hence
The aethereal moon now weds the night
Adorned in the quillets[192] of love's revels.

The sea in thy eyes is yclept[193] heaven:
With price of purest glow and breathing streams
I've bought a dwelling-place where, it seems,
No one draws the curtain on thy face
And pity is a tempest overpast
Weeping, making a doubt,[194] cursing, praising,
Embellishing the ground with grassy bones.

And you smile in that rugged way,
And shiver even as a herd-abandoned hind
Struck by a hunter's flash of light.

The housekeeping[195] of this cloud we call earth
Shall thus anon[196] be over:
But don't wail and scream!
For your unsettled tears are all in vain:
Better change the nimble[197] moans of dirge
Into thy liberal[198] moans of ardent love!

---

[192] Quillets – verbal niceties
[193] Yclept – called
[194] Making a doubt – voicing apprehension
[195] Housekeeping – hospitality
[196] Anon – soon
[197] Nimble – humble
[198] Liberal – unrestrained

The Foretold Hour

The lull'd emotion of the sea's causing
The charmed sky's deliberate pause[199]:
The harmonies of stars, with pliable emotion,
The floating galaxies that perpend[200] on woes
Ne'er before weaved in so much vainglory
Have all gently bowed before thee
So deadly late into the worthied[201] night.

For thy breath outwears thy breast,
And the moon wears out the stars,
And since the light of day returns so soon,
Let the fleshment[202] of this frantic aeon
Have, unsmitten by our sword,
Its foretold very merry hour,
So that the withered blades of grass
Can still grow under the iron soles
Of the smoked[203] and trumpet-blown
Angel of Sorrow that melts the dew on thy brow
And kneels unassumingly before thy shadow.

---

[199] Deliberate pause – something done with much deliberation
[200] Perpend – ponder
[201] Worthied – enhanced with worth
[202] Fleshment – bloodthirstiness
[203] Smoked – hellish; from hell

Unspoken Vow

The place where decay has set its seal
Ripens without[204] the dreamy storm of an instant:
Its wave can slay the better days of a life
And its love, alas, wholly disavow.

Thy beauty though ne'er fades
Even as the morn that follow'd a sad night,
When the brightest star for reasons yet unknown
Fell on this our earth from the high.

So I have one wish left in mine remaining years:
To gaze profoundly on thy countenance,[205]
The most endearing of all things that stay behind,
For death dost not dare consort with it.

And then, what's eternity's recompense,
If not the echoless things it doth amass?
For not e'en the ravined[206] tyranny of time
Could expunge[207] the moonshine of thy breast.

---

[204] Without – outside
[205] Countenance – face
[206] Ravined – ravenous, hungry, starving
[207] Expunge – obliterate, erase, wipe out

When Hearts Are Remembered Not

When hearts are remembered not
And the wintry laughter of life's been heard,
When the unkissed lips no more echoes render
And all those sweet love numbers[208]
Are scattered in the moonshine dust,
When solitude engenders both joy and sorrow,
The allotted hour for the living
Is bound to cease sternly shrouded.[209]

The light of thy countenance[210] I've weaved
Of my darkest woes to thee consecrated;
Yet, thou leavest me to be unforeseen
In thy bosom a face of brass[211] shedding tears,
In my soul the recollection of a midnight yell.

---

[208] Numbers – verses, lines
[209] Sternly shrouded – secretly
[210] Countenance – look, face
[211] Face of brass – brazen-faced man; brave-looking man

Lady Death

Her breath is a blast,
Her pride is the turf,
Her autumn is green,
Her ecstacy[212] sorriest.[213]

The trumpet will blow,
The banners will plummet,
Misshapen, cruel and pale
The future's yet unspoken.[214]

The gold is now withered,
The sea no more parted,
The incarnadined[215] sky
With no dawn or sunset.

Unsmote by the stern gaze
From the enduring throne,
Death, so voluptuous a bride,
Into her sunken bed taketh us.

---

[212] Ecstacy (old spelling with a "c" before "y") – frenzy
[213] Sorriest – most contemptible
[214] Unspoken – unannounced, unknown
[215] Incarnadined – reddened

The Sonnet of Love Past

The flowers and canker of this love past
Are mine alone, a volcanic isle
And a jealous leaf that shall frown betimes[216]
Upon a basilisk's[217] bracing passion.

A fearful hope was all the world contain'd
And the flesh of the dropping dead consum'd:
The wildest wings and the useless brutes
That dispute the rotting love's estates.

And for a moment I am the sullen sky,
Troth-plight[218] to the tombless moon,
The crawling twin of the viper's vows.

The flowers and canker of this love past
Are mine alone, a heart that hardly breathes
So late into the purblind[219] night.

---

[216] Betimes – soon

[217] Basilisk – a mythical serpent-like creature whose look is fatal.

[218] Troth-plight – married

[219] Purblind – completely blind

In the Elysian Fields

I beheld thee mid the land of night,
Equal to the cherubim on high,
A fairy form of starlight sheen[220]
Fading in the unbeaming tears
Of some condoling[221] meadows' winds.

And the future glide is a quiet glacial crypt
Wherein Phibbus[222] hath ne'er eyed the hour,
And the morn's music charmeth not the dark
With melodious sympathies of dole[223]
For the wretched anguish-hearted.

And as thou flee from light to shade in haste,
The wanton[224] winds upon thee play,
Blowing from thy cold unmoving lips
The perfect halo of a final kiss.

---

[220] Starlight sheen – shining starlight
[221] Condoling – lamenting
[222] Phibbus – Phoebus, the sun-god
[223] Dole – grievous event
[224] Wanton – lively, frolicsome, enjoying fun

www.ingramcontent.com/pod-product-compliance
Ingram Content Group UK Ltd.
Pitfield, Milton Keynes, MK11 3LW, UK
UKHW041902190726
13854UKWH00003B/1045

9 781105 570650